LOVE, LOSS, AND EVERYTHING IN BETWEEN

NICOLE LOHER

RISING ACTION

Text copyright © 2025 by Nicole Loher

All rights reserved. For information regarding reproduction in total or in part, contact Rising Action Publishing Co. at http://www.risingactionpublishingco.com

Cover Illustration © Miruna Cucu
Distributed by Simon & Schuster

ISBN: 978-1-998076-80-2
Ebook: 978-1-998076-16-1

POE024000 POETRY / Women Authors
POE023020 POETRY / Subjects & Themes / Love & Erotica
POE023010 POETRY / Subjects & Themes / Death, Grief, Loss

#LoveLossAndEverythingInBetween

Follow Rising Action on our socials!
Twitter: @RAPubCollective
Instagram: @risingactionpublishingco
Tiktok: @risingactionpublishingco

Follow Nicole on Tiktok and Instagram: @nicoleloher

For my partner, Eric, for showing me what love is.

For my sisters, Chelsea, Rose and Maggie, for carrying me through the depths of loss.

For my therapist, Jonathan, for helping me make sense of everything in between.

This collection of poems and prose is an exploratory meditation of healing, resilience, and self-discovery in the wake of profound life changes and hurdles.

Inspired by my personal journey through the heartbreak of a two-year divorce while balancing the unique challenges of completing a Master's degree during a pandemic, I attempted to capture the intense emotions of transition with raw honesty and deep empathy.

A work that has been six years in the making, this collection offers you, my dear readers, a comforting companion on your own path toward a life of ease, a gentle reminder of your strength, and a nudge to seek beauty begging to be found, even in the darkest of times.

I hope however you found these pages, they found you whenever you needed them the most.

Contents

LOVE, LOSS, AND EVERYTHING IN BETWEEN

Love

Love is planting seedlings in the spring, hoping they'll bloom into a garden.

Love is putting trust in the universe that the stars will align.

Love is whispering your desires and hopes to the wind.

Love is having the courage to dream. Big.

Love is doing something over again.

Love is for you, me, them, and us.

Becoming

Admiration and awe
Someone you've never met
But have seen from afar
The truth is
You are her; she is you

The Art of Impermanence

Sometimes is not always
And always isn't forever
Practicing patience is a virtue
Patience, a mind's keepsake
Virtue, a heart's treasure

Bravey

It's okay to start small
It's fine to stand tall
You're allowed to not know it all
What's important is how you rise after each fall
Embrace the journey
Heart and mind, give it your all

Inspired by Alexi Pappas' book, Bravey

"Bravey" is the word for dreaming like crazy. It's for the relentless who replace "can't" with "maybe." The wild dreamers, the unruly risk-takers. Those who can be completely shattered by it all and still see the greatness life has to offer. A beacon of hope that helps them climb their way back to the top. "Bravey" is for those who sprint headfirst into the unknown. The doers, the dreamers, the makers.

For My Girls

Only love for my girls
Sunrise, surf, kisses
Martini nightcaps
Texting each other
"I'm home"
But also
"Can you believe this shit?"

Only love for my girls
Traveling to new places
But eating cereal in bed
Shirley temples for dessert
Jokes of creating our own compound
(Except that's not actually a joke)

Only love for my girls
Unspoken code

Unbroken code:

> I'll drop anything to be right there
> I'm on your side no matter what's been done
> I like all your shared memes because
> It's part of you showing me who you are

Only love for my girls
Because I get them
And they get me
And what more could I wish for
In a life that feels like an eternity?

A Different Perspective

"Not a burden,"
You respond
"But a joy, even a *delight*"

Each word dressed with tenderness
Laced with consideration and care
And your eyes
Flicker with light

A sense of reassurance
Knowing you've told me something
No one else has before
It's home

I know it's true
And I'm meant to be
Right here
With you

When you're in the right company surrounded by aligned love—the kind that makes you feel cared for like we delicately tend to an orchid or a rose requiring full sun and deep watering, a sense of attunement and balance of wants and needs, you will flourish.

Good Morning

You know the feeling is here to stay
When you wake up
And smile at yourself most days

Before there was dread
Now I know
It was all in my head

These days I wake
With clarity
Ease
Purpose
Belonging

Serenity.

Our Race

Not too slow, not too fast
We're eager to remain cautious
We want this to last
Our pasts wrought with pain
One and the same
Light the candle again
A slow-burning flame

You Can Have Both

To love another is fun
To drive with the windows down
Hair tousled, laughs intertwined
To finally catch our breath

With all our cards on the table
Fear set aside
To be completely here
With me

But to love yourself is a joy
An answer that comes without question
A source of strength that nothing can destroy
That no one else can ever take away

Mom,

Everything I am is because of you. I've watched you dedicate your life to teaching others—how to be kind and how to show up—even when you have nothing left to give.

It can't be easy, but you choose to do it anyway. Selfless. I am my mother's daughter, and I will attempt to do the same.

Finding a Home With You

Mundane most of the time,
But so spectacular too
That's the whole point of this:
To know ease
To understand someone else
To wake up unafraid
With steady breaths,
Inhale, exhale
Here and now,

I'm ready
To stay

It was a Wednesday, and like all Wednesdays for the nine months previously, it was date night. Nine months is a long time. But we took things slow, so we were still getting to know each other. We sat in the front booth at Di An Di, exhausted by the day but elated to see each other. We ordered curry, which I spilled all over my only white button-down, and we talked about our day. Unfiltered. No performance. Just going on with no agenda. And that's when you said, "I like this version of you."

4/6

When you said, "I like this version of you"
After I fully showed you myself anew
It takes courage to reveal one's core
To open up and to let one's true self pour

I spent months hiding in my past, cowering out of fear. Too scared of what my actions meant and what you would think. Rejection from divorce, my parents, all the forums. How could I expect you to love me, if I couldn't love me and my closest family chose to exile me?

We were in the 2000s but everyone was acting like we lived in the 1950s. Fear set in and anticipation built as I sat across from you on your leopard-print couch. I paused, dug deep, and I knew I had to tell you if I wanted us to be true.

3/30

The way you held me after I told you about life before
A moment of pause to reflect
You took extra care to intertwine our arms
Then a deep breath
    Inhale
    Exhale
You kissed me
On the forehead
In your favorite spot
And told me you only care about my past
So it could inform our future,
One meant to last

We sit across from each other cross-legged and wide-eyed. We'd dimmed the lights with *our* playlist on in the background. I slowly opened the little red box you got me for Christmas: *We're Not Really Strangers*, different from our weekly General Tso's, wine, and a movie. We played card by card, unveiling confession after confession until we got to the end.

"What's one word to describe our relationship?" the cards posed.

You whispered, " *Comfortable*."

1/29

"Comfortable"
That was the single word
You whispered to describe our relationship
Comfortable
In the way we look at each other
Speak to one another, touch
Comfortable
In the life we're building
And the existence we're maintaining
Comfortable with you

Date/Unknown

We aren't really strangers
A test of faith
An exam of strength
Newly formed, freshly bloomed
Can you recall the question
Of what would we make together?
You said, "A beautiful life.
And art."

Our first tree-trimming party, and all our friends came together at once. You chose the music—Classic Christmas. Bing Crosby, Nat King Cole, Andy Williams. We chose the menu of all French favorites —bœuf bourguignon and Syrah overflowed the room. Our friends cozied up before we all laughed as we decorated. We really set the stage for the words to come:

"I love you" for the first time.

12/4

Seven months
To the day
You looked me in the eyes
In a different way

With your head
Tilted to the side
A soft smile
And trembling lips

You breathed
"I love you."
And I knew because I did too

Warren Street

Skipping down the steps
Of Le Perche
Our favorite place to eat
I look over in your direction
And our hands collided like magnets
And clasped
As we spilled onto the street
You said,
"She's in love"
Then we laughed

This is Life

I no longer ache how I used to
Life now, so sweet
Waking to coffee brewing,
Served to me the way I like it
Serenaded by the complex improvisation
Of jazz coming from the speakers
Comfortable silence in the living room
Because we don't have to speak to each other
To know we're there
Falling asleep to dreamy eyes
Gazing back at me, the real me

Looking Glass

And if nothing else,
Even if we don't last
Or drift apart
I'm thankful you showed me
A new way to love
And to be loved

Today, Yesterday, Tomorrow, Forever

After all this time
Each moment I turn to you
As you do your routine
Wash your face
Brush your teeth
Comb your hair
At half past ten
Every night before bed
I'm still as in love with you
As the first time I laid eyes on you

Ritual of Self

My love for me runs deeper
Than the need to please another
If the world ended tomorrow
I'd be fine being my own lover

To My Brother On His Hardest Days

What a gift it is
To love deeply
To feel alive
To be brave
Isn't it a bit strange
How we exist here at all?
Maybe it's magic

A Legacy of Love

If there's one thing I know
I want for certain in this life
It's to be loved
To feel loved
And to give love

Random phone calls on a Tuesday
Cross-country trips just to spend time
The "I'm so proud of you" texts
Funny memes, especially when
I'm going through a tough time

The legacy of love
Means you imparted
Kindness, patience, and support
Living life on purpose
Leading with grace

No Place Like Home

Home
My sacred place
Where the birds wake
With Dad's first sip of coffee

The deer emerge from the mist
And the sun
Peeks above the misted grass
While Mom swings on the front porch

Home
My sacred place
Where I can just be myself
And rest easy

Verdon Gorge

In a dark place, somewhere in space
Pored over my favorite paperback
Squinting, struggling, still
In my place
You reached up and turned on the light
To illuminate the pages
The darkness was dulled, a subtle act of care
Something normal for you
But a gesture almost too much for me to bear

Loss

Loss can be painful but it can also be liberating. It's a redirection, another chance.

Losing yourself can be catastrophic. How many decisions lead us to become someone we no longer recognize?

Everything that was once secure is now gone. Friday evenings no longer feel comfortable without plans with your someone.

Losing a partner can feel like losing a part of yourself. Everything you've grown into being with another soul evaporates.

Memories become a relic of the past. Or did they even happen?

But what about things we're meant to lose? The people, places, mental keepsakes, and things that no longer serve us? The ones that weigh us down over a lifetime?

To not recognize loss for all its beauty—the perspective it gives you —is a disservice to self.

Time Lost

Do you ever think about me
similar to how I think about you?
My eyes and mind filled
With intrigue
Yours returned adoration

Do you ever detest me
The way I wince when I think about you?
Your glazed-over look
Of disconnect

Do you ever contemplate our past?
We spent so much time together,
I bet you do

Do you remember
How we locked eyes
Before goodbye
For the very last time,
With abandon

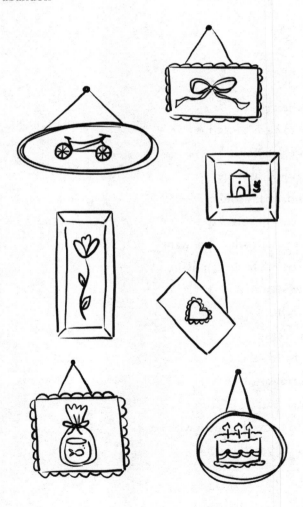

Why Not Me?

I look at others
Who seem to have it together
I can't quite describe it
But it's definitely not me
Sound mind, steady soul
A piqued sense of curiosity
They know exactly what they want
And if they don't have their desire
They know what to do to get it
I look on with envy
Confusion, desire
How can they do that
Without shame, fear?
What in their past
Led them to know their path with ease?
Maybe one day, that'll be me

The Missing Piece

Without you
I don't know who I am
You eased life in a way
I didn't know until
you were gone
My backbone
You gave me a sense of self
But I do know
I will find myself again
Strong as I stand

Here Then Gone

Love is such a strange thing

One day you can have it so concretely,
You know it so well that
It becomes part of you
All of who you are

Love becomes your first thought
Upon waking
It transforms into your life force
Your reason to keep going

It becomes making the bed so
We share something nice at the
Start and end of the day
It's muscle memory

And then suddenly,
Nothing more than a memory
Like a bygone morning,
Time that slipped through the cracks

Who Is She?

Looking in the mirror is always the hardest part
When the person staring back you
Isn't really you anymore
This person you stare at
She's sad
Downcast eyes
Dejected frown
Rounded shoulders
Vacant heart
Yet she holds hope
That it won't always be like this

+you

When it comes down to it,
We're all just fractions
Of all the people we've ever loved,
Or still do

From how we say good morning,
Farewell,
And I love you

When the End is Near

Waking up to someone who doesn't want you
Is much harder
Than waking up alone
The fear of failure, a cemented reality
Desire, replaced with detest
How can one be expected to rest?

In Retrospect:

Outcome: *inevitable*
Heartbreak: *foreseeable*
Words: *irreversible*
Actions: *unspeakable*
Feelings: *deniable*
Outcome: *predictable*

Worthless

What if the worst thing to fear
Is losing yourself
When you've got nothing left?

Our Home

Maybe Mother Earth's just mad at us
The way she comes crashing down
As death tolls rise
Politicians roll their eyes

I can't blame her
In what world is this neglect right?
Our world, only our world
Where money and power win every fight

How long can this last?
An undeniable truth:
She suffers
And we're a moment of her past

Outsider

I'm living in a world
That thrives on "give and take"
No matter what I do
I can't relate
I give everyone my all
And all's what they take
There is no reverse
There is no escape

I can't take your pain away, but I can feel with you.
And sometimes, that's enough.

Citalopram

I can't seem to get my head on straight
Waking up three hours late
I don't know how to find my balance
Or what that even is
I long for the days of normalcy
Knowing everything will be fine
And I can go one day
Where I don't break down and cry

Not seeing someone for who they are is the largest betrayal of human connection.

To: Little Me

Lately, I've been thinking a lot about the little girl
The one with the bowl cut, who was only 5 or 6
When her dad abandoned her in a landfill parking lot
With just a suitcase and tears streaming down her face
She's the same girl who was left behind again
With just a suitcase and tears streaming down her face
While she watched her dad drive off with her brothers
Abandonment never leaves your mind or soul

Lately, I've been thinking a lot about that little girl
Except this time, she's grown, she has a life of her own
When she packs her suitcase now, it's to places unknown

Lately, I've been thinking a lot about that little girl
Except now she's 30, with a home and no longer alone
A chosen family, who would never leave her behind

Lately, I've been thinking a lot about that little girl
The distance between her and me is small
Abandonment never leaves your mind or soul
But eventually, she learned to take care of her

When you grow up with caregivers who don't take care of your needs, you grow into an adult who ignores her own intuition.

Bad Dreams

When the lights go out
My brain follows suit
Shadows of despair
Dreams ripped apart
I can't close my eyes
Corners filled with overwhelming doubt
I can't, I won't ever get out

There's Only Two Truths

Do you ever think about how
You were either the traumatized
Or the traumatizer?
There's a fine line
Between truth and memory

Summiting Everest Alone

How do you love yourself
When no one else loves you?
It's a journey so vast
A pursuit so daunting
Like scaling the world's tallest mountain
One step
One day
One thought
At a time

Sometimes Giving It Your Best Isn't Enough

Sometimes I get angry
When I think back to the downfall of us
My eyes water and my chin quivers

If we only tried a little harder:
  If we communicated better
  If we made love more often
  If you'd just helped me unload the dishwasher
  If I just listened a little more

Could we have made it then? I think so.
But then I remind myself
That's not who we were

   We'd always ignore the big things that needed to be talked about
   We'd always pride ourselves on the fact that we didn't argue
   You'd always pretend like everything's okay
   I'd always go along with the storyline

Our hourglass is spent
There's no going back

Even though I know we're over and done
And it's (probably) for the best
All I can be is angry

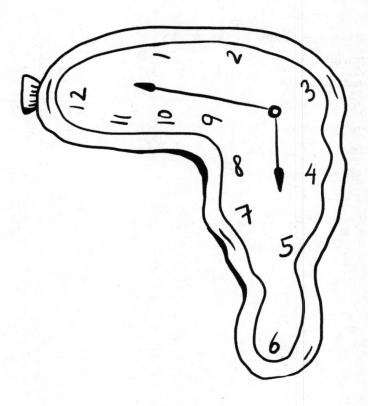

Love Desert

Drinking from a hose
But eyes remain damp
A warm bump
Reduced to tears
A waterfall
But still no end
Distorted and distant
And unsure of what's real
And what's not
In the love desert

Your Passing

A new depth to darkness
The day you departed
It wasn't right
The emptiness in your eyes
Your breath, so shallow
Your passing, it haunts
My life, now hollow

Catastrophic Timelines

Every time you let fear lead
Hope quiets
Uncertainty settles
A loss of self
Each time
It's pain renewed
And worse
It's because of you

Mind Games

I can't remember where we began
I'm not sure where we end
Our lives intertwined
A life tragically upended

You Aren't The Person I Met On Our First Date

I fear what I know
What I've learned about you
Since the beginning
Who you really are
And what you really care about
And what we became
And what we will never be
It's not what you promised

Around Again

Malaise and mundane
It's all the same
My stupid little brain
It can't catch a break

We were less than a year in when you called me *"Boring."* It was expressed out of fear. If we would work, if we moved beyond where we were. The reality was that I wasn't showing up, and you weren't showing out. But we both stayed because we realized nothing is perfect.

Peering Off the Top of Mountains

Standing at the edge of the world
A silent abyss
Do you know what it feels like to be alone
Without you, without me
Life aimless

(Everything In Between)

The thing is, we're always in between.

We're always evolving.

Always learning.

Always growing.

It's part of being human.

It's part of being alive.

The First Day Alone

No one tells you how lonely the first night will be
The quietness you dreamt of is extra loud
The "what ifs" overflow like a full storm drain
And no matter how many friends you can call
They all have to go to sleep at some point
Darkness.

No one tells you how beautiful the next morning feels
The quietness you dreamt of has arrived
The "what ifs" overflow in the form of possibilities
The night before, a fever dream
There's foundation, life to build again
Lightness.

Asking For Help Is The Hardest Part

Sometimes, I'm fine
Most times, I'm not
There are moments when I feel so deeply

My eyes well
And overflow
I can't trust my brain

So I feel with my heart
But what good is living
If the two exist apart

How I Really Feel vs. How I *Really* Feel

Occasionally I might,
But usually, I won't
The fear of me holds me back
And I don't care if I don't

A Lifetime of Pressure

They say you're tough
But your mind feels fragile
You stand tall
But you feel small
There's mounting pressure
To please everyone
On repeat in your brain:
You mustn't be dull

What's Actually Happening?

Looking back and seeing what I thought
     Was wrong with me
     My story
     My life's timing

Wasn't wrong at all
It was all part of my story
That made me, me

Falling down the rabbit hole of
     The time I thought I once
     The potential I dreamt I abandoned
     The memories I attempted to shunned

It was grief
And that's okay
But now it's how it should be

Personal Growth

Short & sweet
Perfectly poised
You're the one they want to meet
But what happens
When you become you
Honest & raw
Full of fire
True to who you are?
Perfectly poised?
I'd say even more

We repeat
What we don't reflect

We repeat
What we don't

We repeat
What we

We repeat
What

We repeat

We repeat

We repeat

Codependent

Fear of the latch
The depending
The anxiety of awaiting
Love of the anchor
The depending
The anticipation of evaporating

Let me ask you something:

What would you do if you could do it all, no wasn't an answer, and you knew you couldn't fail? Who would you see if you could recreate a moment in time, bring a person back once more, and place was irrelevant? Who would you be if you could be anything, if nothing held you back?

A False Fable

It's been said that "time heals all"
But maybe that isn't true
Maybe it's all the self-work and thinking and reflection
That one has to do
But even when you're healed
Your life's simply renewed

There are few instances in which
You'd call your own daughter weak
The first being
Describing her physical being,
Merely as a temporary ailment
In fact, that is the only time

You shouldn't call your daughter weak when
She left a marriage
That was not good for her
The same marriage she chose
Because she had you as a role model

As she spent her younger years
Searching for love and acceptance
You seem to have forgotten
All your weak daughter overcame

Your daughter isn't weak
She's the strongest

How do you say hello when you've been gone for so long? Existing on a different plane, subsisting at a different frequency. How do you make amends with the people you once loved? Your absence certainly didn't make their hearts grow fonder. How do you show up again? When who you are now isn't who they remember you as?

Ready or Not

Are you ready to put it all down
To drop the rope
To sink in, dig your heels deep
To be who you need to be
To say goodbye to who you no longer are
All for the sake of who you want to become
Are you ready?

Dear Self

In not so long you'll feel so relieved
Food will taste better
Colors will look bolder
Sounds will hum brighter
Life will feel lighter

Keep going

What We Didn't Learn

When safety is masked as boring
Fear arises
You look for reasons to point fingers
Fight to cause commotion
Just because that's what you're used to
Within a chaotic house,
Where nothing is safe
And your mind can't be sound
Normality ensues

Sometimes the things that are supposed to keep us safe suffocate us the most, ultimately derailing our growth, stopping us from who we want to be.

A Fine Line

Life could go in so many ways
But how does one balance the tension
Of decision and fate
When do you know to go with the flow
How do you learn to course-correct?
Maybe we never do
Maybe that's life
Maybe it's something we'll regret

You don't just learn to love again. It's a process, built on a bedrock of shared trust over time. The best part is, if you can wait just long enough, all will be sublime.

A Waiting Game

I can't be the only one
Who imagines life as a countdown
Things can be good, golden even
But pain lurks around the corner
Catastrophizing
It's overwhelming, exhausting
A smile for a moment
But bracing for the inevitable

Tell Me, What Are We Doing Here?

A dance of emotions, we sway and wane
In this hazy realm of exhilaration and aching
I can't unravel the path we're on
Lost in the fray, yet not quite gone

A Relationship From Broken Homes

Daily thoughts
When nothing's taught
Nothing's learned
Two souls turned
Eight years past
It would never last

Fear raised me. The trauma of someone who survived womanhood in the 1950s. The same woman who couldn't own property, make contracts or get divorced, and had no say over her earnings.

She was encouraged to be a homemaker, to make men feel nice (even when they weren't at all kind) because they held the keys to her future.

I too hold that panic but I also lean into freedom. Because I refuse to allow dread to control me.

The End

At the world's collapse
My brain starts to wander
What will you think about?
What will consume your last breath?
Because I can only think of you

What Are We?

The moments between
Knowing and unknowing
What we are and what we aren't
Who I am and who you are
And who I'm not and who you aren't
It could be clarified with delicate words
But fear holds us back
And our emotions, conceal

The Space Between

Think with your brain
Feel with your heart
More often than not
These two are worlds apart
Competing for space,
Feelings and pace
It's hard to tell where one ends
And the other starts

Unsteady Ground

Nothing is permanent
Everything is uncertain
A warm hand
Heartbreak's cure

To See Again

After darkness
You never forget
What the first glimpse of light looks like
Hope.

Otherworldly

On what planet
Is being smaller
Better?

In the past,
We hid
To survive

Luckily, that's
No longer
Our world

Broken Infinity Sign

When you end and I begin
The feelings meld
What world do we live in?
An endless circle
A broken fragment of one
I'm not quite sure
When we said "done"

As I look to the future with refreshed eyes, I now realize that everything is *in between*.

In life, there is no start and end except for birth and death, and the rest is a dream.

If you take one thing from me, make it this: Each day when you wake up, know that you can begin again.

Acknowledgments

First and foremost, I want to thank Alexandria and Tina for believing in me enough to publish me without ever publishing poetry before! That is crazy! And to the entire Rising Action team —Abby, Miruna, Sarah, and the Simon & Schuster family—thank you for your support throughout this process.

As an extension of that, Molly Burford, my incredible editor and friend: you have no idea how much your guidance meant to me in this procses. I can't believe we met on Tumblr and now get to work together! Thank you from the bottom of my heart.

Kara Cutruzzula—thank you for not laughing at me when I cold emailed you to ask if I could hire you to help me write my first query letter. And you agreed! You are my favorite author of all time so to have your support and expertise in crafting this book means the world. Thank you, friend.

I also want to acknowledge my friends, Brian and Karina—the first two people to congratulate and celebrate with me as soon as I found out this book would be published. You brought me the nicest bottle of wine that I ended up saving until on mine and Eric's last night of living in New York. I will never forget how loved and supported I felt that day from you two. You are top tier friends.

My therapist, Jonathan: Thank you for taking my dreams and joys seriously, and caring about how I am. It has taught me how to take care of myself—physically, mentally, creatively and spiritually. This book was once my biggest dream and today it is my biggest reality, all because you encouraged me.

To my partner, Eric. I hope we get a million lifetimes together. You are the greatest thing to ever happen to me and you helped heal a part of me I didn't think could be healed. I love you so much.

And finally, to my sisters: Chelsea, Rose and Maggie. Dedicating this book wasn't enough. The endless calls, shared memes, late night texts, bottles of wine and french fries, screaming into the void while holding each other's hand, ten minute rambling voice notes, FaceTimes...thank you. I love each of you to the moon and back. You're my soulmates.

About the Author

Nicole Loher is an award-winning communications strategist, researcher, and adjunct professor at New York University. Her work sits at the intersection of insights, strategy and emerging technology to help tell stories that advance complex communications goals. Her work has received multiple awards, has been recognized in trade press, and is featured in the Smithsonian.

As the founder of Climate Communications Collective, a boutique firm focusing on the intersection of climate and all forms of communication, Nicole spends her days supporting organizations that are committed to advancing society. craft better communications that resonate in an increasingly chaotic communications landscape.

Nicole has also spent the last decade teaching at New York University. During her tenure, she led the creation and development of the school's first social media course curriculum, is the lead principle for white papers at the intersection of sustainability and communications, and wrote the school's first climate communications course, which will debut in Fall 2025.

Nicole is currently working on her second book, *Going Through It*.